Spilled Milk

Written by Mark Siswick

Illustrated by Mike Phillips

Collins

That morning, the mist was so thick!
Farmer Jon was hoisting milk churns
on to the trailer.

The trailer tipped up, the churns burst and milk swooshed into the mud. Clatter! Bang!

"That's a reet mess! This milk is spoiled," groaned Jon.

"Now then, Mark and Fee, help me get the rest of the milk to the shop."

4

Mark frowned, then turned to Fee and said, "The green boat! It's in the barn!"

5

The children hoisted the milk into
the boat and started to drag it down
the steep bank to the river.

The mist was so thick ... Bump!
The boat hit something – Dot the cow!

The boat rocked as it floated down the river. Dot mooed in alarm.

The mist thickened.

Fee thrust out her hand into the gloom and grabbed ... an astonished hen!

Flap!

Cluck!

The little green boat *was* crowded!
But the end was in sight.

With a mammoth spurt of power, the children strained to pull the milk churn up the steep bank.

They were smeared with mud as they staggered into the shop.

But the shopkeeper grinned – she was delighted with the milk.

Milk trip

🐾 Review: After reading 🐾

Use your assessment from hearing the children read to choose any GPCs, words or tricky words that need additional practice.

Read 1: Decoding

- Point to **astonished** on page 9. Ask the children: How can you tell that the hen is astonished? (*it flaps and clucks.*)
- Ask the children to sound out and blend these words, identifying the letters that make the long vowel sound:

  gloom   **steep**   **crowded**   **strained**   **smeared**   **floated**

- Read pages 10 and 11 to the children, and explain that you blended the words in your head and not out loud. Challenge the children to do the same, and read the pages, blending in their heads as they read the words.

Read 2: Prosody

- Turn to pages 2 and 3, and focus on words that sound like their meaning:
  - Point to **hoisting**. Say: Read this word in a way that shows the effort in lifting and moving the heavy churns.
  - Point to **burst**. Say: Read this word in a way that sounds like the churns exploding open.
  - Point to **swooshed**. Say: Read this word in a way that sounds like the milk pouring into the mud.
- Challenge the children to read both pages with expression, and remind them to read the sound words (**clatter**, **bang**), too.

Read 3: Comprehension

- Ask the children if they have ever been on a farm, or seen farmers or farm animals on TV programmes. Focus on children's experiences linked to dairy farming and milk.
- Reread page 4 and talk about what the children have to do, and why. (e.g. *They have to take the milk to the shop because the trailer broke.*)
- Challenge the children to retell what happened on the children's journey from the farm to the shop. Prompt with questions about the picture on pages 14 and 15. Ask:
  - What happened on the steep bank outside the farm? (e.g. *they dragged the boat down and hit Dot the cow*)
  - Point to the hen on page 15 and ask: What happened here? (e.g. *Fee grabbed the hen, and it got in to the boat*)
  - Who was in the boat at the end of the journey? (*Mark, Fee, Dot the cow, the hen*)
  - Point to the shop. Ask: How did the children look when they got to the shop? (*muddy*)